Fun With Free-Form Crochet™

By Margaret Hubert

General Information

Many of the products used in this pattern book can be purchased from local craft, fabric and variety stores or from the Annie's Attic Needlecraft Catalog *(see Customer Service information on page 23)*.

Contents

How to Free-Form Crochet

Writing instructions for free-form crochet is certainly a contradiction in terms. By its very name, free-form indicates the absence of instructions. In my many years of teaching, I have found that beginners like to have a little instruction to get started.

Once they have tried the method, their own imagination begins to take over. Soon they are creating the most wonderful things on their own. It is a phenomenon that 12 students given the same set of instructions for a free-form scrumble will come up with 12 different pieces.

On a recent trip to Australia, for a fiber festival, I had the good fortune to take a workshop with James Walters. James and Sylvia Cosh wrote several books on free-form and are credited with coining the word "scrumble." Scrumble is what we call the small pieces that go into creating free-form fabric. I never knew that I was "scrumbling" till I "met" James and Sylvia through their books. I always did my own thing, never knowing the method had a name.

Technically, a scrumble is a random piece of crochet work that uses a combination of stitches, usually different yarns and colors, in a multidirectional way. A motif is a set manner of working a group of stitches. For the purpose of this book, and to be able to write instructions, I have used many motifs, rather than true scrumbles. By combining a few scrumbles with motifs and using them together in an imaginative way, I have tried to create a free-form look and feel to the projects.

It is my hope that readers will take some of the ideas and work with them, add their own innovations and soon become as passionate about free-form crochet as I am.

In my work, I mostly use three methods to create my free-form projects. I use a template as a guide, I use lining, or I use a mesh background and embellish it to create a free-form style. For the projects in this book, I use mainly the lining and mesh methods. They range from easy to moderate to more challenging. As in all free-form crochet, assembly is required. Most of all, have fun; a whole new world of creativity is waiting for you.❏❏

How to Use This Book

There are eight projects in this book: a jacket using the sweatshirt method as a lining; a vest, a capelet and an accent rug using the mesh method; and a pillow, slippers, gloves and two small wall hangings using some innovative ideas in free-form. It is interesting to note that the slippers and the wall hangings use the same Limpet Scrumble.

The Template Method
A template may be made from fabric or poster board. In this method, a shape is either drawn on the poster board or traced on fabric and cut out. The template is a guide; as you make the pieces of crochet, either pin them to the fabric or lay them on the poster board so that you can see the item take shape before sewing the pieces together.

The Lining Method
In this method, the lining becomes part of the finished item. The crochet pieces are sewn to each other and to the lining, not just pinned as in the template method. To create the pillow, I used a pillow form and sewed the pieces to the pillow. For the jacket, I purchased an inexpensive sweatshirt and sewed the crochet pieces to the shirt. When sewing your pieces to the lining, use a sewing needle and matching strong dual-duty thread. When sewing the pieces to each other, use a tapestry needle and matching yarn.

The Mesh Method
An open-work stitch known as filet crochet is usually used to create a lighter, more airy piece. An item is made, either totally or partially in this open-work method, then the area is embellished with motifs. The vest was made in this manner.

The capelet was made by combining individual motifs into clusters, working several rows of picot mesh stitches around each individual cluster before sewing clusters together.

I've included descriptions and given specific yarns, crochet hooks, motifs and stitches used for each piece. Unless changes

Large Paisley Scrumble No. 1

Row 1 (RS): Ch 25, sc in second ch from hook and in each of next 5 chs, hdc in each of next 6 chs, dc in each of next 11 chs, 5 dc in last ch, working on opposite side of ch, dc in each of next 5 chs, hdc in next ch, sc in next ch, sl st in next ch **changing to next color** *(see Stitch Guide)* leaving rem chs unworked, turn. Fasten off first color. *(36 sts)*

Row 2: Ch 1, sc in each of first 8 sts, 2 sc in each of next 5 sts, sc in each st across changing to second color, turn. *(41 sts)*

Row 3: Ch 1, sc in each of first 10 sts, hdc in each of next 10 sts, dc in each of next 6 sts, 2 dc in each of next 5 sts, dc in each of next 5 sts, hdc in each of next 5 sts, sc in each of next 3 chs of row 1, turn. *(49 sts)*

Row 4: Ch 1, sc in each of next 14 sts, [2 dc in next st, dc in next st] 5 times, sc in each st across, changing to next color in last st, turn. *(54 sts)*

Row 5: Working in back lps, ch 1, sc in each of first 27 sts, [2 sc in next st, sc in each of next 2 sts] 5 times, sc in each st across with sc in each of next 2 chs of row 1, turn. *(61 sts)*

Row 6: Ch 1, sc in each of first 22 sts, [2 sc in next st, sc in each of next 3 sts] 5 times, sc in each st across changing to first color in last st made, turn. *(66 sts)*

Row 7: Ch 1, sc in each of first 3 sts, sk next 2 unworked lps on row 4, dc in next lp, sk st behind dc just made, [sc in each of next 3 sts, sk next 2 unworked lps on row 4, dc in next lp, sk next st behind last dc] across with

---

sc in last 2 sts, sc in each of next 2 chs on row 1, **do not turn**. *(73 sts)*

Row 8: Ch 1, working from left to right, **reverse sc** *(see illustration on page 4)* in each st across. Fasten off.

Large Paisley Scrumble No. 2

Row 1 (RS): With first color, ch 25, sc in second ch from hook and in each of next 5 chs, hdc in each of next 6 chs, dc in each of next 11 chs, 5 dc in last ch, working on opposite side of ch, dc in each of next 5 chs, hdc in next ch, sc in next ch, sl st in next ch leaving rem chs unworked, turn. *(36 sts)*

Row 2: Ch 1, sc in each of first 8 sts, 2 sc in each of next 5 sts, sc in each st across **changing to second color** *(see Stitch Guide)*, turn. *(41 sts)*

Row 3: Ch 1, sc in each of first 10 sts, hdc in each of next 10 sts, dc in each of next 6 sts, 2 dc in each of next 5 sts, dc in each of next 5 sts, hdc in each of next 5 sts, sc in each of next 3 chs of row 1, turn. *(49 sts)*

Row 4: Ch 1, sc in first st, hdc in next st, dc in each of next 12 sts, 2 dc in each of next 8 sts, dc in each of next 6 sts, hdc in each of next 14 sts, sc in each st across changing to next color in last st, turn. *(57 sts)*

Row 5: Working in **back lps** *(see Stitch Guide)*, sc in each of first 3 sts, hdc in each of next 10 sts, dc in each of next 15 sts, [2 dc in next st, dc in next st] 6 times, dc in each of next 10 sts, hdc in each st and in each unworked ch of row 1 across, turn. *(75 sts)*

Row 6: Working in **front lps** *(see Stitch Guide)*, ch 1, sc in each of first 7 sts, hdc in each of next 14 sts, dc in each of next 7 sts, [2 dc in next st, dc in each of next 2 sts] 5 times, dc in each st across changing to first color in last st, turn. *(80 sts)*

Row 7: Working in back lps, ch 1, sc in each of first 35 sts, [2 sc in next st, sc in each of next 3 sts] 4 times, sc in each st across changing to second color in last st, turn. *(84 sts)*

Row 8: Ch 1, sc in each of first 33 sts, 3 sc in next st, sc in each of next 18 sts, 3 sc in next st, sc in each st across. Fasten off. *(88 sts)*

Limpet Scrumble

Rnd 1: With first color, ch 4, sl st in first ch to form ring, ch 1, 14 sc in ring, join with sl st in first sc. *(14 sc)*

Row 2: Ch 3 *(counts as first dc)*, dc in same st, 2 dc in each of next 8 sts **changing to next color** *(see Stitch Guide)* in last st leaving rem sts unworked, drop first color, **do not turn.** *(18 dc)*

Row 3: Sk first 10 dc, join second color with sc in next st, sc in same st, 2 sc in each of next 7 dc, tr in each unworked st on row 1, turn. *(22 sts)*

Row 4: Ch 1, sc in each st across changing to first color in last st, turn.

Row 5: Ch 1, sc in each of first 3 sts, 2 sc in next st, [sc in each of next 3 sts, 2 sc in next st] 4 times, sc in each of last 2 sts, turn. *(27 sc)*

Row 6: Ch 1, *limpet st *(see Special Stitches on page 4),* rep from * 5 times, sc in each st across changing to second color in last st, turn.

Row 7: Ch 3 *(counts as first st),* dc in each of next 2 sts, 2 dc in next st, [dc in each of next 3 sts, 2 dc in next st] 3 times, 2 dc in each sc between limpet sts, 2 dc in last st changing to first color in last st, turn. Fasten off second color. *(42 dc)*

Row 8: Ch 1, sc in first st, [sk next 2 sts, 5 dc in next st, sk next 2 sts, sc in next st] 6 times, sk next 2 sts, 5 dc in next st, sk next st, sc in last st. Fasten off.

Mock Popcorn Scrumble

Notes: *When corners are formed by making 3 sts in same st, the center st of these 3 sts always becomes corner st on next row.*

When changing colors, always change in last st made (see Stitch Guide).

Row 1: With first color, ch 10, sc in second ch from hook, sc in each ch across, turn. *(9 sc)*

Row 2: Ch 3 *(counts as first dc),* dc in each of next 3 sts, sc in each st across **changing to next color** *(see Notes),* turn. Fasten off first color.

Row 3: Working in **back lps** *(see Stitch Guide),* ch 1, sc in each of first 5 sts, hdc in next st, dc in each st across, turn.

Row 4: Working in back lps, ch 3, sc in same st, (tr, sc) in each st across changing to next color, turn.

Row 5: Working in unworked lps of row 3, ch 1, sc in each of first 3 sts, hdc in each of next 2 sts, dc in each st across, turn.

Row 6: Ch 1, sc in each st across changing to second color, turn.

Row 7: Working in back lps, ch 1, sc in each st across with 3 sc in last st *(corner made),* working in ends of rows, sc in end of each row across, turn. *(17 sc)*

Row 8: Working in back lps, ch 3, sc in same st, (tr, sc) in each st across changing to third color, turn. Fasten off second color.

Row 9: Working in rem lps of row 7, ch 1, sc in each of first 3 sts, hdc in each of next 3 sts, dc in each of next 3 sts, 3 dc in corner st, dc in each st across, turn. *(19 sts)*

Row 10: Ch 1, sc in each st across with 3 sc in corner st changing to next color, turn. Fasten off last color. *(21 sc)*

Row 11: Ch 1, sc in each st across to corner st, (sc, hdc, dc) in corner st, dc in each st across, turn. *(23 sts)*

Row 12: Working in back lps, ch 1, sl st in each st across changing to next color, turn. Fasten off last color.

Row 13: Working in rem lps of row 11, ch 1, sc in each of first 5 sts, hdc in each of next 5 sts, dc in each st across to corner, 3 dc in corner st, dc in each st across, turn. *(25 sts)*

with 3 sc in corner st, sc in each st across changing to first color, turn. Fasten off last color. *(27 sc)*

Row 15: Working in back lps, ch 1, sc in each of first 5 sts, hdc in each of next 5 sts, hdc in each st across to corner, 3 dc in corner st, dc in each st across, turn. *(29 sts)*

Row 16: Ch 1, sl st in each st across. Fasten off.

Curly-Edge Leaf
SPECIAL STITCH

Picot: Ch 3, sc in third ch from hook.

Rnd 1: Ch 16, sc in second ch from hook and in each ch across with 3 sc in last ch, working on opposite side of ch, sc in each ch across, **do not join or turn**. *(33 sc)*

Rnd 2: Working in **back lps** *(see Stitch Guide),* sc in next st, [**picot** *(see Special Stitch),* sl st in next st, sc in next st] 7 times, sc in next st, picot, sl st in next st *(point of leaf made),* [picot, sl st in next st, sc in next st] across, sl st in last st, sl st in end of row, for **stem,** ch 12, sc in second ch from hook, sc in each ch across, sl st in end of next row on leaf. Fasten off.

Broad Leaf
Row 1: Ch 15, 5 tr in fifth ch from hook, tr in each of next 3 chs, dc in each of next 3 chs, hdc in each of next 3 chs, (sc, ch 3, sc)

in last ch, working on opposite side of ch, hdc in each of next 3 chs, dc in each of next 3 chs, tr in each of next 3 chs, 6 tr in last ch, turn. *(32 sts)*

Row 2: Ch 3 *(counts as first dc),* dc in each of next 10 sts, hdc in each of next 4 sts, sc in next st, (sc, ch 3, sc) in ch sp, sc in next st, hdc in each of next 4 sts, dc in each of next 11 sts, ch 2, sl st in same st as last dc. Fasten off.

Single Crochet Leaf

Row 1: Ch 2, 3 sc in second ch from hook, turn. *(3 sc)*

Row 2: Ch 1, 2 sc in first st, sc in next st, 2 sc in last st, turn. *(5 sc)*

Row 3: Ch 1, 2 sc in first st, sc in each st across with 2 sc in last st, turn. *(7 sc)*

Row 4: Ch 1, sc in each st across, turn.

Row 5: Ch 1, **sc dec** *(see Stitch Guide)* in first 2 sts, sc in each of next 3 sts, sc dec in last 2 sts, turn. *(5 sc)*

Row 6: Ch 1, sc dec in first 2 sts, sc in next st, sc dec in last 2 sts, turn. *(3 sc)*

Row 7: Ch 1, sc dec in next 3 sts,. Fasten off.

Small Leaf

Ch 12, 5 dc in fourth ch from hook, dc in each of next 4 chs, hdc in each of next 2 chs, sc in next ch, (sc, ch 3, sc) in last ch, working on opposite side of ch, sc in next ch, hdc in each of next 2 chs, dc in each of next 4 chs, 5 dc in last ch, ch 3, sl st in same st as last dc. Fasten off.

Large Leaf

Row 1: Ch 16, 5 dc in fourth ch from hook, dc in each of next 7 chs, hdc in each of next 3 chs, sc in next ch, (sc, ch 3, sc) in last ch, working on opposite side of ch, sc in next ch, hdc in each of next 3 chs, dc in each of next 7 chs, 6 dc in last ch, turn. *(36 sts)*

Row 2: Ch 3, dc in same st, dc in each of next 9 sts, hdc in each of next 5 sts, sc in each of next 3 sts, (sc, ch 3, sc) in ch sp, sc in next 3 sts, hdc in each of next 5 sts, dc in each of last 10 sts, ch 3, sl st in same st as last dc. Fasten off.

Ridged Leaf

Row 1: Ch 12, sc in second ch from hook, sc in each of next 9 chs, 5 sc in last ch; working on opposite side of ch, sc in each of next 7 chs leaving rem chs unworked, turn. *(22 sc)*

Note: *Work in back lps unless otherwise stated.*

Row 2: Ch 1, working in **back lps** *(see Note),* sc in each of first 9 sts, 3 sc in next st, sc in each of next 9 sts leaving rem sts unworked, turn. *(21 sc)*

Row 3: Ch 1, sc in each of first 10 sts, 3 sc in next st, sc in each of next 8 sts leaving rem sts unworked, turn.

Row 4: Ch 1, sc in each of first 9 sts, 3 sc in next st, sc in each of next 9 sts leaving rem sts unworked, turn.

Row 5: Ch 1, sc in each of next 10 sts, 3 sc in next st, sc in each of next 8 sts leaving rem sts unworked, turn.

Row 6: Ch 1, sc in each of first 9 sts, 3 sc in next st, sc in each of next 9 sts leaving rem sts unworked, turn.

Row 7: Ch 1, sc in each of next 10 sts, 3 sc in next st, sc in each of next 8 sts leaving rem sts unworked, turn.

Row 8: Ch 1, sc in each of first 9 sts, 3 sc in next st, sc in each of next 9 sts leaving rem sts unworked, turn.

Row 9: Ch 1, sc in each of first 10 sts, 3 sc in next st, sc in each of last 10 sts. Fasten off.

Small Plain Triangle

Row 1: Ch 13, sc in second ch from hook and in each ch across, turn. *(12 sc)*

Rows 2–5: Ch 1, sk first st, sc in each st across, turn, ending with 8 sc.

Row 6: Ch 1, **sc dec** *(see Stitch Guide)* in first 2 sts, sc in each of next 4 sts, **sc dec** in last 2 sts, turn. *(6 sc)*

Row 7: Ch 1, sc in each st across, turn.

Row 8: Ch 1, **sc dec** in first 2 sts, sc in each of next 2 sts, **sc dec** in last 2 sts, tog, turn. *(4 sc)*

Row 9: Ch 1, sc in each st across, turn.

Row 10: Ch 1, **sc dec** in first 2 sts, **sc dec** in last 2 sts, turn. *(2 sc)*

Row 11: Ch 1, sc in each st across, turn.

Row 12: Ch 1, **sc dec** in first 2 sts. Fasten off.

Decorative Triangle

Rnd 1: Ch 6, sl st in first ch to form ring, ch 4 *(counts as dc, ch 1)*, dc in ring, ch 2, [dc, ch 1, dc, ch 2] in ring 5 times, join with sl st in third ch of first ch-4. *(12 dc, 6 ch-1 sps, 6 ch-2 sps)*

Rnd 2: Ch 1, [sc in next ch-1 sp, (dc, ch 1, dc, ch 1, dc) in next ch-2

sp] around, join with sl st in first sc. *(18 dc, 6 sc, 12 ch-1 sps)*

Rnd 3: Ch 4, *[sc in next ch-1 sp, ch 1] twice, (dc, ch 1, dc, ch 5, dc, ch 1, dc) in next sc *(corner made)*, [ch 1, sc in next ch-1 sp] twice**, ch 1, dc in next sc, ch 1, rep from *, ending last rep at **, join with sl st in third ch of ch-4. Fasten off.

3-Circle Motif

Row 1: Ch 5, sl st in first ch to form ring, ch 3 *(counts as first dc)*, 13 dc in ring, turn. *(14 dc)*

Row 2: Ch 1, sc in each of first 2 sts, [ch 1, sc in each of next 2 sts] 6 times, turn.

Row 3: Ch 6, sl st in first ch sp *(second ring made)* leaving rem ch sps unworked, turn.

Row 4: Ch 3, 13 dc in second ring, sl st in first sc of first ring, turn.

Row 5: Ch 1, sc in each of first 2 dc, [ch 6, sc in each of next 2 dc] 6 times, sl st in next ch-6 sp on last ring, turn.

Row 6: Ch 6, sl st in first ch-6 sp *(third ring made)*, turn.

Row 7: Ch 3, 13 dc in last ring made, turn.

Row 8: Ch 1, sc in each of first 2 dc, [ch 6, sc in each of next 2 dc] across. Fasten off.

Chrysanthemum

Rnd 1: Ch 5, sl st in first ch to form ring, ch 1, 8 sc in ring, join with sl st in first sc. *(8 sc)*

Rnd 2: Ch 3 *(counts as first dc)*, dc in same st, 2 dc in each st around, join with sl st in top of ch-3. *(16 dc)*

Rnd 3: Working in **front lps** *(see*

Stitch Guide), ch 1, sc in first st, ch 5, [sc in next st, ch 5] around, join.

Rnd 4: Working in rem lps of rnd 2, ch 1, sc in first st, ch 7, [sc in next st, ch 7] around, join. Fasten off.

8-Petal Daisy

Rnd 1: Ch 4, sl st in first ch to form ring, ch 1, 8 sc in ring, join with sl st in first sc. *(8 sc)*

Rnd 2: Working in **back lps** *(see Stitch Guide)*, ch 8, [sc in next st, ch 8] around, join with sl st in joining sl st of last rnd.

Rnd 3: Ch 1, 10 sc in each ch sp around, join. Fasten off.

SMALL FILL-INS
Shell Fill-in

Ch 3, 6 dc in third ch from hook, ch 2, sl st in same ch, pull end tight, ch 3, 6 dc in same ch, ch 3, sl st in same ch. Fasten off.

Circle Fill-in

Ch 4, sl st in first ch to form ring, ch 3 *(counts as first dc)*, 12 dc in ring, join with sl st in top of ch-3. Fasten off.

Mock Popcorn Flower

Rnd 1 (RS): Ch 5, sl st in first ch to form ring, ch 1, 8 sc in ring, join with sl st in first sc. *(8 sc)*

Rnd 2: Ch 1, 2 sc in each st around, join, turn. *(16 sc)*

Rnd 3 (WS): Ch 3, sc in same st, (tr, sc) in each st around, join with sl st in top of ch-3, turn.

Rnd 4 (RS): Ch 1, working in tr only, [3 dc in next tr, ch 1, sl st in next tr, ch 1] around, join with sl st in joining sl st of last rnd. Fasten off.

Small Flower Fill-in

Rnd 1: Ch 4, sl st in first ch to form ring, ch 1, 10 sc in ring, join with sl st in first sc. *(10 sc)*

Rnd 2: Ch 3, 3 dc in next st, ch 3, [sl st in next st, ch 3, 3 dc in next

st, ch 3] around, join with sl st in joining sl st. Fasten off.

Large Flower Fill-in

Rnd 1: Ch 4, sl st in first ch to form ring, ch 1, 10 sc in ring, join with sl st in first sc. *(10 sc)*

Rnd 2: Ch 3, 5 tr in next st, ch 3, [sl st in next st, ch 3, 5 tr in next st, ch 3] around, join with sl st in joining sl st. Fasten off.

3-Petal Violet

Ch 4, sl st in first ch to form ring, (ch 2, dc, tr, ch 3, sc in third ch from hook, tr, dc, ch 2, sl st) in ring 3 times. Fasten off.

Tunisian Stitch With Shells

Row 1: Ch 28, 4 dc in fourth ch from hook *(first 3 chs count as dc)*, sk next 3 chs, sc in next ch, sk next 3 chs, [9 dc in next ch, sk next 3 chs, sc in next ch, sk next 3 chs] twice, 5 dc in last ch, turn.

Row 2: Ch 1, sc in first st, *[pull up lp in next st, hold lp on hook] 5 times *(6 lps on hook)*, pull up lp in next st and pull this lp through first lp on hook forming bar, [yo, pull through 2 lps on hook] 5 times *(6 bars and 1 lp on hook)*, **the lp on hook counts as first st, so sk first bar, hold lps on hook, pull up lp in each of next 5 bars *(6 lps on hook)*, pull up lp in next st and through first lp on hook, [yo, pull through 2 lps] 5 times, rep from ** twice, insert hook in second bar, yo, pull through bar and lp on hook *(one st bound off)*, bind off 4 more sts, sc in next st, rep from * ending bind off 5 sts, sl st in top of last st, turn.

Row 3: Ch 1, sc in first st and in each st across, turn.

Row 4: Yo, pull up lp in second st, yo, pull through 2 lps on hook, [yo, pull up lp in next st, yo, pull through 2 lps on hook] 3 times, yo, pull all 5 lps on hook, ch 1 tightly for eye of shell, *ch 3, sc in next st, ch 3, [yo, pull up lp in next st, yo, pull through 2 lps on hook] 9 times, yo, pull through 10 lps on hook, ch 1 tightly to form eye of shell, rep from * ending last rep with [yo, pull up lp in next st, yo, pull through 2 lps on hook] 4 times, yo, pull through 5 lps on hook, ch 1 tightly to form eye, turn.

Row 5: Ch 3, 4 dc in eye of first shell, sc in next sc, [9 dc in eye of next shell, sc in next sc] across ending with 5 dc in eye of last shell, turn.

Row 6: Rep row 2. Fasten off.

For larger piece, rep rows 2–5 as desired.❑❑

SKILL LEVEL

INTERMEDIATE

FINISHED SIZE
Adult size

MATERIALS
- ❑ Berroco Glace fine (sport) weight yarn (1¾ oz/75 yds/ 50g per hank):
    - 10 hanks #2003 taupe
- ❑ Size G/6/4mm crochet hook
- ❑ Tapestry needle

PATTERN NOTE
Capelet is made by first making up a cluster of Motifs, working mesh stitches around each cluster, then sewing the clusters together.

INSTRUCTIONS

Large Leaf Cluster (make 4)
For each Cluster, make three Large Leaves *(instructions are on page 7)*, three Large Flower Fill-ins *(instructions are on page 9)*.

Arrange the flowers and leaves in a group, having two Clusters with the flowers and leaves graduating up at a slant to the right, two going to the left.

When flowers and leaves are sewn tog, join with sl st in any side st and work mesh picot st around entire Cluster as follows:

Rnd 1: *Ch 5, sk next 4 sts, sc in next st *(when working the first row around flowers, ch 5, sk from petal

to petal, when working leaves at points, ch 5, go back into same st)*, rep from * evenly spaced around, join with sl st in first sl st.

Rnds 2 & 3: *Ch 5, for **picot** (sc, ch 3, sc) in next ch sp, rep from * around, join. At end of last rnd, fasten off.

Ridged Leaf Cluster (make 2)
For each Cluster, make three Ridged Leaves *(instructions are on page 7)*.

When leaves are made, sew tog from top to about first ridge.

Join yarn in any st at top and work three rnds of picot mesh evenly spaced around entire cluster as in Large Leaf Cluster.

Curly-Edge Leaf (make 22)
Rnd 1: Ch 16, sc in second ch from hook and in each ch across with 3 sc in last ch, working on opposite side of ch, sc in each ch across, **do not join or turn.** *(33 sc)*

Rnd 2: Working in **back lps** *(see Stitch Guide)*, ch 1, sc in next st, [ch 3, sc in third ch from hook *(picot made)*, sl st in next st, sc in next st] 7 times, sc in next st, picot, sl st in next st *(point of leaf made)*, [picot, sl st in next st, sc in next st] across, sl st in next st. Fasten off.

FINISHING
Arrange Clusters having two Large Clusters tog, a Ridged Leaf Cluster, two Large Leaf Clusters, and a Ridged Leaf Cluster, joining to form Capelet, as shown in photo.

When Clusters are joined, join with sl st in any side st, form neckline as follows:

Rnd 1: *Ch 5, sk next 4 sts, sc in next st, rep from * around, join with sl st in first sl st.

Rnds 2 & 3: [Ch 5, (sc, ch 3, sc) in next ch sp] around, join.

Rnds 4 & 5: (Ch 3, sc, ch 3, sc) in each ch sp around, ch 3, join. At end of last rnd, fasten off.

Sew 11 Curly-Edge Leaves along the bottom edges of each Ridged Leaf Cluster, sewing only the top of the leaf and letting rem hang down like fringe.❑❑

Color Me Purple Sweatshirt Jacket

SKILL LEVEL
INTERMEDIATE

FINISHED SIZE
Medium size shown

MATERIALS FOR MEDIUM SIZE ONLY
- ❑ Lion Brand Wool-Ease Sport fine (sport) weight yarn (5 oz/435 yds/140g skein):
    - 2 skeins #144 purple *(A)*
    - 1 skein #148 turquoise *(A)*
- ❑ Lion Brand Micro Spun fine (sport) weight yarn (2½ oz/ 168 yds/70g per skein):
    - 3 skeins #147 purple *(B)*
    - 1 skein #148 turquoise *(B)*
    - 1 skein #144 lilac
    - 1 skein #143 lavender
- ❑ Lion Brand Fun Fur bulky (chunky) weight eyelash yarn (1¾ oz/60 yds/50g per skein):
    - 2 skeins #191 violet
- ❑ Lion Brand Watercolors fine (sport) weight yarn (1¾ oz/55 yds/50g per skein):
    - 1 skein #347 purple haze
- ❑ Sizes H/8/5mm, I/9/5.5m and J/10/6mm crochet hooks
- ❑ Bent-end tapestry needle
- ❑ Sewing needle
- ❑ Thread
- ❑ 7 (¾-inch) buttons
- ❑ Medium-size purple sweatshirt

SWEATSHIRT
1. Cut off neck band, waistband and cuffs.

2. Lay sweatshirt flat, measure a center front line, mark with pins or quilter's pencil, then cut along this line.

3. Turn sweatshirt inside out. Sew scrumbles to the fleece side, leaving the finished smooth side as jacket lining.

PATTERN NOTES
For small or larger sizes adjust yarn amounts.

Begin making crochet pieces. First, pin in place; then, using a tapestry needle, sew several pieces to each other, then sew pieces to sweatshirt using sewing needle and thread. Continue in this way, working with only three or four pieces at a time. I usually start at the neckline and work my way down. For this garment, I worked very simple triangles to lie flat under the collar.

Using a sweatshirt makes a very heavy jacket. If you do not want such a heavy garment, you can use the sweatshirt as a template. Just baste your scrumbles to the sweatshirt, then sew them to each other. When the entire piece is done, cut the basting stitches and remove the lining *(sweatshirt)*. You will have the shape without the weight.

Dye lots are not important in free-form crochet; you can always buy more yarn to add if needed.

Use H hook unless otherwise stated.

INSTRUCTIONS
Half-Circle Shell Motif *(instructions on page 4)*
Make two using purple A as first color, turquoise B as second color, lilac as third color and lavender as fourth color.

Make one using purple A as first color, purple B as second color, lilac as third color and lavender as fourth color.

Make one using purple A as first color, purple B as second color, lilac as third color and purple B as fourth color.

Make one using purple A for first, second and third colors and purple B for fourth color.

Curly-Edge Leaf *(instructions on page 6)*
Make two using turquoise A.
Make four using purple A.
Make one using lilac.
Make one using turquoise B.

Small Flower Fill-in *(instructions on page 9)*
Make six using purple A.
Make 10 using purple B.
Make five using lilac.
Make three using turquoise B.
Make two using lavender.
Make one using turquoise A.

Small Leaf *(instructions on page 7)*
Make five using purple A.
Make three using purple B.
Make two using turquoise B.

Large Leaf *(instructions on page 7)*
Make three using purple A.
Make two using purple B.
Make two using turquoise B.

Crescent *(make 5)*
With I hook and purple haze, ch 12, 2 dc in third ch from hook and in each ch across. Fasten off.

Lazy-J Scrumble
(instructions on page 4)
Make six using purple A as first color, purple B as second color lilac as third color and lavender as fourth color.

Shell Fill-in
(instructions on page 8)
Make three using purple B.
Make three using purple A.

3-Circle Motif
(instructions on page 8)
Make one using purple A.
Make one using purple B.
Make one turquoise B.

Small Plain Triangle
(instructions on page 8)
Make 12 using purple A.
Make 12 using purple B.
Make four using lilac.
Make two using purple haze.

Background Fan
Make 6 using purple A as first color and purple B as second color.
Make 2 using lilac as first color and purple A as second color.
Make 2 using purple B as first color and purple A as second color.
Make 2 using purple A as first color and turquoise B as second color.
Rnd 1: Ch 4, sl st in first ch to form ring, ch 1, 14 sc in ring, join with sl st in first sc. *(14 sc)*
Row 2: Ch 3 (counts as first dc), dc in same st, 2 dc in each of next 8 sts leaving rem sts unworked, **do not turn.** Fasten off. *(18 dc)*
Row 3: Sk first 10 dc, join next color with sc in next st, sc in same st, 2 sc in each of next 7 dc, tr in each unworked st on rnd 1, turn. *(22 sts)*
Row 4: Ch 1, sc in each st across **changing to first color** *(see Stitch Guide)* in last st, turn.
Row 5: Ch 1, sc in each of first 3 sts, 2 sc in next st, [sc in each of next 3 sts, 2 sc in next st] 4 times, sc in each of last 2 sts, turn. *(27 sc)*
Row 6: Ch 3, dc in each of next 2 sc, [2 dc in next st, dc in each of next 4 sts] across with 3 dc in last st changing to

second color, turn. Fasten off first color.
Row 7: Ch 1, sc in first st, [ch 3, sc in third ch from hook, sc in each of next 2 sts] across. Fasten off.

Chain Loop Fill-in (make 3 purple A and 3 purple B)
Row 1: Ch 19, sc in second ch from hook and in each ch across, turn. *(18 sc)*
Row 2: Ch 1, sc in each st across, turn.
Row 3: Working in **back lps** *(see Stitch Guide)*, ch 1, sc in first 2 sts, [ch 6, sc in each of next 2 sts] across. Fasten off.

Ridged Leaf
(instructions on page 7)
Make three using purple A.
Make three using purple B.

Limpet Scrumble
(instructions on page 5)
Make five using purple A as first color, lavender as second color and turquoise B as third color.
Make two using purple A as first color and purple B as second and third colors.

5-Petal Roll Flower
(instructions on page 4)
Make two using purple B.
Make one using purple A.
Make one using turquoise B.

Decorative Triangle
(instructions on page 8)
Make four using purple A.
Make four using purple B.

Large Paisley Scrumble No. 1
(instructions on page 5)
Make two using purple A as first color, lavender as second color and turquoise A as third color.
Make two using purple A as first color, lilac as second color and turquoise A as third color.

Large Paisley Scrumble No. 2
(instructions on page 5)
Make two using purple A as first color, lilac as second color, purple B as third color and turquoise A as fourth color.

Mock Popcorn Scrumble
(instructions on page 6)
Make two using purple A for first color, purple B as second color, turquoise B as third color, lavender as fourth color and purple haze for fifth color.
Make five using purple A as all colors.
Make two using purple haze as first, second, third and fourth colors and purple A as fifth color.

Mesh Fill-in (make 2 purple A of each size)
Notes: *In order to have less bulk in the under area, I use lightweight mesh pieces to fill in. The large is used on the sleeve underarm, the small and medium used to fill in where needed.*
Pattern is written for small size with medium and large sizes in [ ].
Row 1: Ch 13 [15, 17], dc in fourth ch from hook and in each ch across, turn. *(11 [13, 15] dc)*
Rows 2–5 [5, 7]: Ch 3, dc in each st across, turn.
Row 6 [6, 8]: Ch 3, dc next 2 sts tog, dc in each st across to last 2 sts, dc last 2 sts tog, turn.
Next rows: Rep rows 2–6 [6, 8] consecutively until 3 [3, 5] sts rem. Fasten off on small and medium sizes only.
Next rows: Large size only, work even until piece fits from wrist to underarm when slightly stretched. At end of last row, fasten off.

COLLAR
Row 1: With size I hook and purple haze, ch 74, sc in second ch from hook and in each ch across, turn *(73 sc)*
Row 2: With size J hook, ch 1, sc in each st across, turn.
Next rows: Rep row 2 until piece measures 3½ inches or more. At end of last row, fasten off.

Left Front Button Border
Row 1: Starting at top front edge, RS facing, using color of your choice, evenly sp sc, being sure sts lie flat, turn.
Rows 2–5: Ch 1, sc in each st across, turn. At end of last row, fasten off.

Mark this side for seven evenly spaced buttons.

Right Front Buttonhole Border
Row 1. Starting at bottom front edge, RS facing, using color of your choice, evenly sp sc being sure sts lie flat, turn.

Row 2: Ch 1, sc in each st across, turn.

Row 3: Using marked side as guide, ch 1, [sc in each st across to marker, ch 2, sk next 2 sts] 7 times, sc in each st across, turn.

Row 4: Ch 1, sc in each st and ch across, do not turn. Fasten off.

Row 5: With RS facing, join with sc in last st, working from left to right, **reverse sc** *(see illustration)* across. Fasten off.

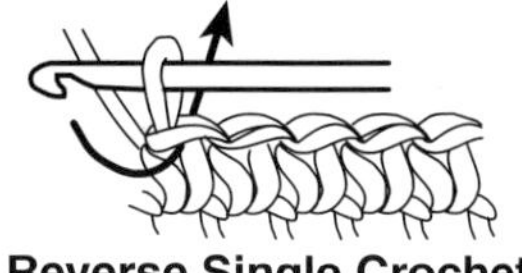

Reverse Single Crochet

FINISHING
Using J hook and purple haze, work one row of surface sc diagonally across Right Front and starting on Left Front so that the diagonal line continues. Work a row of sc diagonally across back and each sleeve.

Mark center back of neck and center of Button Bands, fold Collar in half, pin center of Collar to center back of neck, having front edges of Collar ends at center of Button Bands, ease Collar, pin and sew in place.❑❑

Garden Patch Accent Rug

SKILL LEVEL

INTERMEDIATE

FINISHED SIZE
24 x 28 inches

MATERIALS
❑ Patons Astra fine (sport) weight yarn:
- 3½ oz/266 yds/100g #2881 forest green
- 3½ oz/266 yds/100g #2217 country green
- 1¾ oz/133 yds/50g #2939 kelly green
- 1¾ oz/133 yds/50g #2941 school bus yellow
- 1¾ oz/133 yds/50g #0081 golden yellow
- 1¾ oz/133 yds/50g #2895 lipstick pink
- 1¾ oz/133 yds/50g #2223 crayon red
- 1¾ oz/133 yds/50g #2752 baby pink
- 1¾ oz/133 yds/50g #2740 purple
- 1¾ oz/133 yds/50g #8328 violet
- 1¾ oz/133 yds/50g #8728 hot fuchsia
- 1¾ oz/133 yds/50g #2901 deep orange
- 1¾ oz/133 yds/50g #8714 mango
- 1¾ oz/133 yds/50g #2763 copen blue
- 1¾ oz/133 yds/50g #2783 aran
- 1¾ oz/133 yds/50g #2913 cocoa
- 1¾ oz/133 yds/50g #2765 black

❑ Sizes E/4/3.5mm and G/6/4mm crochet hooks
❑ Bent-end tapestry needle
❑ 2 ladybug buttons (optional)
❑ 24 x 28-inch piece rug canvas

PATTERN NOTES
When ending each motif, leave a long end for sewing. Following photo or placing motifs in an arrangement pleasing to you, sew into place, sewing into the large holes in canvas.

Use G hook unless otherwise stated.

INSTRUCTIONS
Large Leaf
(instructions on page 7)
Make 10 using kelly green.
Make eight using country green.
Make 10 using forest.

Small Leaf
(instructions on page 7)
Make five using kelly green.
Make five using country green.
Make five using forest.

Curly-Edge Leaf
(instructions on page 6)
Make two using kelly green.
Make eight using country green.
Make four using cocoa.
Make four using forest.

Broad Leaf
(instructions on page 6)
Make two using kelly green.
Make one using country green.
Make five using forest.

Chrysanthemum
(instructions on page 8)
Make two using school bus yellow.

Forget-Me-Not (make 6)
Rnd 1: With golden yellow, ch 4, sl st in first ch to form ring, ch 1, 10 sc in ring **changing to copen blue** *(see Stitch Guide)* in last st made, join with sl st in first sc. Fasten off yellow. *(10 sc)*

Rnd 2: Ch 3, 3 dc in next st, ch 3, [sl st in next st, ch 3, 3 dc in next st, ch 3] around, join with sl st in joining sl st. Fasten off.

3-Petal Violet
(instructions on page 9)
Make six using violet.

8-Petal Daisy
(instructions on page 8)
Make three using hot fuchsia.

Poppy (make 1)
Rnd 1: With deep orange, ch 4, sl st in first ch to form ring, ch 1, 8 sc in ring, join with sl st in first sc. Fasten off. *(8 sc)*
Rnd 2: Working in **front lps** *(see Stitch Guide)*, join black with sl st in any st, ch 1, dc in first st, 2 dc in next st, [dc in next st, 2 dc in next st] around, join with sl st in first dc. *(12 dc)*
Rnd 3: Ch 2, [sl st in next st, ch 2] around, join with sl st in joining sl st. Fasten off.
Rnd 4: Working in rem lps of rnd 1, join mango with sl st in any st, 2 dc in first st and in each st around, join. *(24 dc)*
Rnd 5: Ch 3 *(counts as first st)*, 2 dc in next st, [dc in next st, 2 dc in next st] around, join. *(36 dc)*
Rnd 6: Ch 3, dc in each of next 2 sts, 2 dc in next st, [dc in each of next 3 sts, 2 dc in next st] around, join. *(45 dc)*
Rnd 7: Ch 3, dc in each of next 4 sts, 2 dc in next st, [dc in each of next 4 sts, 2 dc in next st] around, join. *(54 dc)*
Rnd 8: Ch 1, sc in first st, hdc in next st, 2 dc in next st, hdc in next st, [sc in each of next 2 sts, hdc in next st, 2 dc in next st, hdc in next st] around, join. *(65 sts)*
Rnd 9: [Ch 2, sl st in next st] around, join with sl st in joining sl st. Fasten off.

Mock Popcorn Flower (instructions on page 9)
Make one using purple.

Shell Fill-in (instructions on page 8)
Make two using purple.
Make three using golden yellow.
Make two using school bus yellow.
Make four using deep orange.
Make two using mango.
Make two using lipstick pink.
Make two using baby pink.
Make two using copen blue.
Make two using hot fuchsia.
Make two using aran.
Make two using crayon red.

Large Flower Fill-in (instructions on page 9)
Make three using mango.

Make three using baby pink.

Buttercup (make 3 school bus yellow)
Rnd 1: Ch 4, sl st in first ch to form ring, ch 1, 8 sc in ring, join with sl st in first sc. *(8 sc)*
Rnd 2: Ch 1, 2 sc in each st around, join. *(16 sc)*
Rnds 3–5: Ch 1, sc in each st around, join.
Rnd 6: Sl st in each st around, join with sl st in first sl st. Fasten off.

Bluebell (make 3 copen blue)
Rnd 1: Ch 4, sl st in first ch to form ring, ch 1, 8 sc in ring, join with sl st in first sc. *(8 sc)*
Rnd 2: Ch 1, 2 sc in each st around, join. *(16 sc)*
Rnds 3–5: Ch 1, sc in each st around, join.
Rnd 6: Working from left to right, **reverse sc** *(see illustration)* in each st around, join. Fasten off.

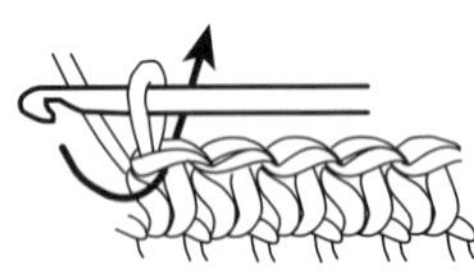

Reverse Single Crochet

Delphinium Cluster (make 3 violet, 3 purple, 3 hot fuchsia)
Ch 4, 5 dc in fourth ch from hook, ch 2, sl st in same ch *(petal made)*, [ch 6, 5 dc in fourth ch from hook, ch 2, sl st in same ch] 5 times *(total of six petals)*, working on opposite side of petals just made, sc in base of next petal, [ch 3, 5 dc in same ch, ch 2, sl st in same ch, sc in base of next petal] 5 times. Fasten off.

Pink Canterbury Bell (make 3 baby pink)
Rnd 1: Ch 4, sl st in first ch to form ring, ch 1, 8 sc in ring, join with sl st in first sc. *(8 sc)*
Rnd 2: Ch 1, 2 sc in each st around, join. *(16 sc)*
Rnds 3–5: Ch 1, sc in each st around, join.
Rnd 6: Ch 1, sc in first st, [hdc in next st, dc in next st, sc in each of next 2 sts] around ending last rep with sc in last st, join. Fasten off.

Mock Popcorn Fern (make 2)
Row 1: With forest, ch 15, sc in second ch from hook, sc in each of next 2 chs, hdc in each of next 4 chs, dc in each of last 7 chs, turn. *(14 sts)*
Row 2: Working in **back lps** *(see Stitch Guide)*, ch 3 *(counts as first tr)*, sc in same st, (tr, sc) in each st across **changing to kelly green** *(see Stitch Guide)* in last st made turn.
Row 3: Working in rem lps of row 1, ch 1, sc in each of first 3 sts, hdc in each of next 4 sts, dc in each of last 7 sts, turn.
Row 4: Rep row 2 changing to country green in last st.
Row 5: Rep row 3.
Row 6: Rep row 2 do not change colors. Fasten off.

Pansy
Make 2 with purple centers and golden yellow petals.
Make 3 with golden yellow centers and aran petals.
Make 2 with cocoa centers and golden yellow petals.
Rnd 1: For **center**, ch 4, sl st in first ch to form ring, ch 1, [sc, ch 3] 5 times in ring, join with sl st in first sc **changing to petal color** *(see Stitch Guide)*. Fasten off. *(5 ch-3 sps)*
Rnd 2: For **petals**, ch 1, (sc, ch 1, 4 dc, ch 1, sl st) in each of next 2 ch sps *(large petals)*, (sc, 3 hdc, sl st) in each of next 3 ch sps.
Rnd 3: Working on large petals only, [sl st in ch-1, 2 sc in each of next 4 dc, sl st in ch-1, sc in ch-3 sp] twice. Fasten off.

Black-Eyed Susan (make 2)
Rnd 1: With golden yellow, ch 4, sl st in first ch to form ring, ch 1, 14 sc in ring, join with sl st in first sc. *(14 sc)*
Rnd 2: For **petals**, [ch 10, sl st in second ch from hook, sc in next ch, hdc in each ch across, sl st in next sc on rnd 1] around. Fasten off. *(14 petals)*
Rnd 3: For **center**, with size E hook and cocoa, ch 2, 4 sc in second ch from hook, join with sl st in first sc. *(4 sc)*

Rnd 4: Ch 1, 2 sc in each st around, join. Leaving a long end, fasten off.

Weave long end back through top of sts, pull to form dome. Sew to center of petals.

Daisy (make 2)
Rnd 1: With aran, ch 4, sl st in first ch to form ring, ch 1, 10 sc in ring, join with sl st in first sc. *(10 sc)*

Rnd 2: For **petals,** [ch 8, sl st in second ch from hook, sc in next ch, hdc in each ch across, sl st in next sc on rnd 1] around. Fasten off. *(10 petals)*

Rnd 3: For **center,** with size E hook and golden yellow, ch 2, 4 sc in second ch from hook, join with sl st in first sc. *(4 sc)*

Rnd 4: Ch 1, 2 sc in each st around, join. Leaving a long end, fasten off.

Weave long end back through top of sts, pull to form dome. Sew to center of petals.

Pinecone Flower (make 2)
Work Daisy using lipstick pink for petals and cocoa for center.

Small Flower Fill-in
(instructions on page 9)
Make five using golden yellow.

Make six using golden yellow as center and aran as petals.

Make six using lipstick pink.

Make eight using golden yellow as center and crayon red as petals.

Make six using violet.

Shell Fill-in
(instructions on page 8)
Make four using deep orange.

Make two using mango.

Make two using purple.

Make three using school bus yellow.

Make three using golden yellow.

Make two using baby pink.

Make two using lipstick pink.

Make two using hot fuchsia.

Make two using copen blue.

Make two using crayon red.

Make two using aran.❏❏

Purple Power Pillow

FINISHED SIZE
12 inches square

MATERIALS
- ❏ Lion Brand Thick & Quick Chenille super bulky (super chunky) weight yarn:
  6 oz/100 yds/106g
  #146 dark purple
- ❏ Lion Brand Polarspun bulky (chunky) weight yarn:
  1¾ oz/137 yds/50g
  #147 purple
- ❏ Lion Brand Wool-Ease Sport fine (sport) weight yarn:
  5 oz/435 yds/140g
  #144 purple
- ❏ Lion Brand Microspun fine (sport) weight yarn:
  2½ oz/168 yds/70g
  #147 purple
- ❏ Size K/10½/6.5mm crochet hook
- ❏ Bent-end tapestry needle
- ❏ Sewing needle and thread
- ❏ 14-inch square piece of fabric lining
- ❏ 12-inch pillow form

INSTRUCTIONS

Pillow Back
Row 1: With Chenille, ch 28, sc in second ch from hook and in each ch across, turn. *(27 sc)*

Row 2: Ch 1, sc in each st across, turn.

Next row: Rep row 2 until piece measures 13 inches. At end of last row, fasten off.

Pillow Front
Sew lining fabric to pillow form, turning under 1 inch around edges. This lining allows you to sew pieces to pillow and not be concerned if all your pieces do not match up exactly.

Small Plain Triangle (instructions on page 8)
Make four using Wool-Ease.

3-Circle Motif (instructions on page 8)
Make three using Wool-Ease.
Make two using Microspun.
Make one using Chenille.

Curly-Edge Leaf (instructions on page 6)
Make three using Wool-Ease.
Make three using Microspun.

Tunisian and Shells (make 1 Microspun)
Row 1: Ch 60, 4 dc in fourth ch from hook *(first 3-chs count as dc)*, sk next 3 chs, sc in next ch, sk next 3 chs, [9 dc in next ch, sk next 3 chs, sc in next ch, sk next 3 chs] across ending with 5 dc in last ch, turn.

Row 2: Ch 1, sc in first st, *[pull up lp in next st, hold lp on hook] 5 times *(6 lps on hook)*, pull up lp in next st and pull this lp through first lp on hook forming upright st or bar, [yo, pull through 2 lps on hook] 5 times *(6 bars and 1 lp on hook)*, **the lp on hook counts as first st, first bar, hold lps on hook, pull up lp in each of next 5 bars *(6 lps on hook)*, pull up lp in next st and through first lp on hook, [yo, pull through 2 lps] 5 times, rep from ** twice, insert hook in second bar, yo, pull through bar and lp on hook *(one st bound off)*, bind off 4 more sts, sc in next st, rep from * ending bind off 5 sts, sl st in top of last st, turn.

Row 3: Working in **back lps** *(see

Stitch Guide), ch 3 *(counts as first tr),* sc in same st, (tr, sc) in each st across, turn.

Row 4: Working in rem lps of row 2, ch 3, dc in each st across. Fasten off.

Row 5: With RS facing, join Polarspun with sc in first st, sc in each st across. Fasten off.

Circle Fill-in
(instructions on page 9)
Make three using Chenille.
Make three using Polarspun.

Make three using Wool-Ease.

Arrange all motifs on the pillow front as shown in photo or using your imagination. Sew in place.❑❑

<hr>

So Easy Slippers

SKILL LEVEL

INTERMEDIATE

MATERIALS
- ❑ Patons Astra fine (sport) weight yarn (1¾ oz/133 yds/50g per ball):
    - 1 ball #2774 medium blue
    - 1 ball #2753 sky
- ❑ Patons Twister bulky (chunky) weight eyelash yarn (1¾ oz/47 yds/50g per ball):
    - 1 ball #5735 bongo blue
- ❑ Size G/6/4mm crochet hook
- ❑ Clover Doll Making needle
- ❑ 2 La Mode fashion buttons
- ❑ Small package 6mm blue beads
- ❑ Matching thread
- ❑ Pair terry cloth slippers

INSTRUCTIONS
Limpet Scrumble
(instructions on page 5)
Make two using sky as first color and bongo blue as second color and medium blue as third color.

Shell Fill-in
(instructions on page 8)
Make eight using sky.
Make eight using medium blue.

Arrange Limpet Scrumbles on each toe, and sew in place. Then using the Shell Fill-ins, sew to top and side of slippers until covered. Embellish with beads and buttons.❑❑

SKILL LEVEL

INTERMEDIATE

FINISHED SIZES
Ladies 32- to 34-inch bust *(small)*; 34- to 36-inch bust *(medium)*; 36- to 38-inch bust *(large)*; 38- to 40-inch bust *(X-large)*
Pattern is written for small size with larger sizes in [ ].

FINISHED GARMENT MESUREMENTS
34¾ [37¼, 40, 42½] inches

MATERIALS
❑ Patons Astra fine (sport) weight yarn (1¾ oz/133 yds/50g per ball):
  2 [2, 3, 3] balls #88113 denim mix ombre
  1 [1, 1, 1] ball #2763 copen blue
  1 [1, 1, 1] ball #2774 medium blue
  1 [1, 1, 1] ball #2733 electric blue
  1 [1, 1, 1] ball #2753 sky
❑ Size G/6/4mm crochet hook or size needed to obtain gauge
❑ Tapestry needle
❑ Package simulated pearls from Create a Craft

GAUGE
7 dc and 6 ch-2 sps = 4 inches

INSTRUCTIONS

Vest
Note: *Vest is worked in one piece to armholes.*
Row 1: With ombre, ch 159 [171, 183, 195], dc in sixth ch from hook *(count as dc and ch-2)*, [ch 2, sk next 2 chs, dc in next ch] across, turn. *(52 [56, 60, 64] ch-2 sps)*
Row 2: Ch 5 *(counts as dc, ch 2)*, dc in next dc, [ch 2, dc in next dc] across, turn.
Next rows: Rep row 2 until piece measures 6 [6½, 7, 7½] inches from beg.

Right Front
Next row: Ch 5, dc in next dc, [ch 2, dc in next dc] 11 [12, 13, 14] times leaving rem sts unworked, turn. *(12 [13, 14, 15] ch sps)*
Dec row: For **dec**, ch 3 *(does not count as st)*, dc in next st, [ch 2, dc in next st] across, turn. *(11 [12, 13, 14] ch sps)*
Next row: Ch 5, dc in next st, [ch 2, dc in next st] across, turn.
Next rows: Rep dec row and last row alternately until you have 5 [5, 6, 6] ch sps rem.
Next rows: Work even until armhole is 11 [11½, 12, 12½] inches. At end of last row, fasten off.

Left Front
Next row: Starting at underarm, sk next 28 [30, 32, 34] ch sps, join with sl st in next st, ch 3, dc in next dc, [ch 2, dc in next st] across, turn. *(11 [12, 13, 14] ch sps)*
Next rows: Rep Right Front reversing shaping.

Back
Next row: Sk next 2 ch sps, join with sl st in st at right underarm, ch 5, dc in next dc, work in pattern within 2 ch sps of left armhole, turn. *(24 [26, 28, 30] ch sps)*
Next rows: Work dec row twice. *(22 [24, 28, 30] ch sps)*
Next rows: Work even to match Fronts. At end of last row, fasten off.
Sew shoulder seams.

Trim
Row 1: Working across fronts and neck edge, with RS facing, join with sc at bottom edge of Right Front, evenly space sc so sts lie flat across to bottom of Left Front, **do not turn.**
Row 2: Working from left to right, **reverse sc** *(see illustration)* in each st across. Fasten off.

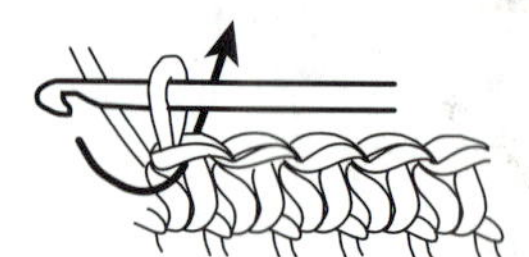

Reverse Single Crochet

Work Trim around each armhole.

EMBELLISHMENTS
Forget-Me-Not (make 2 copen blue, 2 med blue, 2 sky)
Rnd 1: Ch 4, sl st in first ch to form ring, ch 1, 10 sc in ring, join with sl st in first sc. *(10 sc)*
Rnd 2: Ch 3, 3 dc in next st, ch 3, [sl st in next st, ch 3, 3 dc in next st, ch 3] around, join with sl st in joining sl st. Fasten off.

Bluebell (make 2)
Rnd 1: With med blue, ch 4, sl st in first ch to form ring, ch 1, 8 sc in ring, join with sl st in first sc. *(8 sc)*
Rnd 2: Ch 1, 2 sc in each st around, join. *(16 sc)*
Rnds 3–6: Ch 1, sc in each st around, join.
Rnd 7: Ch 1, sc in first st, sk next st, 5 dc in next st, [sk next 2 sts, sc in next st, sk next 2 sts, 5 dc in next st] 2 times, sk last st, join. Fasten off.

Large Leaf (instructions on page 7)
Make three using copen blue.
Make three using electric blue.

Small Leaf (instructions on page 7)
Make six using copen blue.
Make six using electric blue.
Make six using sky.
Make six using medium blue.

3-Petal Violet (instructions on page 9)
Make seven using sky.

Sew to Vest as shown in photo or as desired.❑❑

Butterfly & Flower Wall Hangings

SKILL LEVEL

INTERMEDIATE

MATERIALS
- ❑ Patons Astra fine (sport) weight yarn:
  1¾ oz/133 yds/50g
  #2783 aran
- ❑ Size G/6/4mm crochet hook
- ❑ 2 (8½ x 11-inch) shadow box frames

INSTRUCTIONS

Butterfly

Make two Limpet Scrumbles using one color *(instructions are on page 5).*

Place curved edges tog in shadow box to form Butterfly.

Make two twisted cords as follows: Cut 18-inch length of yarn, fold in half, anchor one end firmly, then twist the two strands very tightly tog, not letting go of either end, fold again and let twist. Tie the loose ends tog. Place between wings, hiding the knotted ends.

Flower

Row 1 (RS): Ch 11, sc in second ch from hook and in each ch across, turn. *(10 sc)*

Row 2: Ch 3 *(counts as first st),* dc in same st, 2 dc in each st across, turn. *(20 dc)*

Row 3: Ch 18, dc in third ch from hook, dc in each of last 15 chs leaving rem sts unworked, turn.

Row 4: Ch 1, work 5 **embossed pockets** *(see Special Stitches on page 4)* across, turn.

Row 5: Ch 2 *(does not count as st),* dc along top of pockets, work dc in each sl st and each sk st, dc in each st across row 2, turn.

Row 6: Ch 2, [**popcorn** *(see Special Stitches on page 4),* sk next st] 5 times, **roll st** *(see Special Stitches on page 4)* across to beg of pockets, working in dc behind pockets, make 5 pockets, turn.

Row 7: Ch 2, dc in each sk st and in each sl st to beg of roll sts, work 2 sc behind the bar of each roll st, turn.

Row 8: Ch 1, sc in first st, 5 dc in next st *(shell made),* [sk next 2 sts, sc in next st, sk next st, 5 dc in next st] across ending with 5 dc in next st, sk next 2 sts, sc in last st, **do not turn.**

Row 9: Working in end of rows, evenly sp sc across rows, working on opposite side of ch on row 3 and starting ch of row 1, evenly sp sc across, turn.

Row 10: Ch 3, sc in same st, (tr, sc) in each st across to shells. Fasten off.

Row 11: With RS facing, join with sl st in first st at beg of row 8, ch 3, dc in same st, [working behind shell, 2 dc in sk st before and after shell *(there are 2 sk sts before the shell, work only in the one right next to shell)*] across row 8 only, turn.

Row 12: Ch 1, sc in first st, [ch 6, sc in next st] across. Fasten off.

Place Flower in rem shadow box frame.❑❑

SKILL LEVEL

INTERMEDIATE

MATERIALS

- ❑ Patons Astra fine (sport) weight yarn:
  - 1¾ oz/133 yds/50g #2913 cocoa
  - 1¾ oz/133 yds/50g #2783 aran
  - ½ oz/38 yds/14g #2765 black
- ❑ Size E/4/3.5mm crochet hook
- ❑ Tapestry needle

INSTRUCTIONS

Small Motif (make 4 aran, 4 cocoa, 2 black)

Row 1: Ch 5, sl st in first ch to form ring, ch 5 *(counts as first dc and ch-2)*, dc in ring, [ch 2, dc in ring] 4 times, turn. *(6 dc made)*

Row 2: Ch 1, sc in first st, [ch 6, sc in next st] across. Fasten off.

Tiny Flowers (make 10 cocoa, 4 aran)

Ch 4, sl st in first ch to form ring, [ch 2, 2 dc, ch 2, sl st] in ring 5 times. Fasten off. *(5 petals made)*

Sew motifs around cuff and part of hand as shown in photo or as desired. ❑❑

Annie's Attic®

306 East Parr Road
Berne, IN 46711
© 2004 Annie's Attic

ISBN: 1-59635-015-6   All rights reserved   Printed in USA   2 3 4 5 6 7 8 9

Stitch Guide

ABBREVIATIONS

beg ....begin/beginning
bpdc ....back post double crochet
bpsc .... back post single crochet
bptr ....back post treble crochet
CC ....contrasting color
ch ....chain stitch
ch- ....refers to chain or space
previously made (i.e. ch-1 space)
ch sp ....chain space
cl ....cluster
cm ....centimeter(s)
dc ....double crochet
dec ..decrease/decreases/decreasing
dtr .... double treble crochet
fpdc .... front post double crochet
fpsc .... front post single crochet
fptr ....front post treble crochet
g ....grams
hdc ....half double crochet
lp(s) ....loop(s)
MC .... main color
mm .... millimeter(s)
oz ....ounce(s)
pc .... popcorn
rem ....remain/remaining
rep .... repeat(s)
rnd(s) .... round(s)
RS ....right side
sc .... single crochet
sk ....skip(ped)
sl st ....slip stitch
sp(s) ....space(s)
st(s) ....stitch(es)
tog ....together
tr ....treble crochet
trtr ....triple treble
WS .... wrong side
yd(s) ....yard(s)
yo ....yarn over

Chain—ch: Yo, pull through lp on hook.

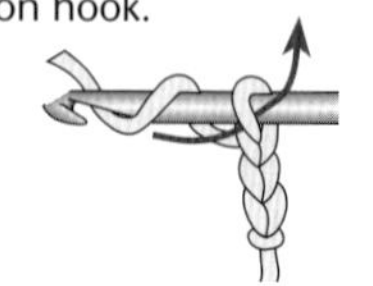

Slip stitch—sl st: Insert hook in st, yo, pull through both lps on hook.

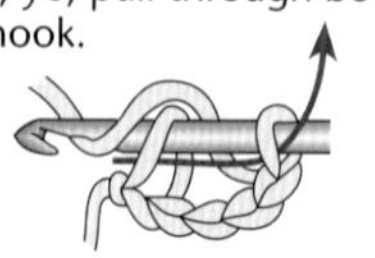

Single crochet—sc: Insert hook in st, yo, pull through st, yo, pull through both lps on hook.

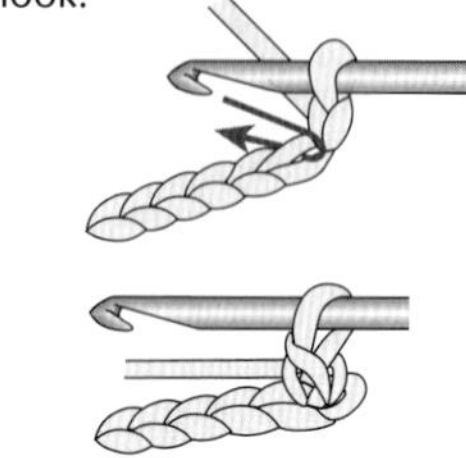

Front loop—front lp
Back loop—back lp

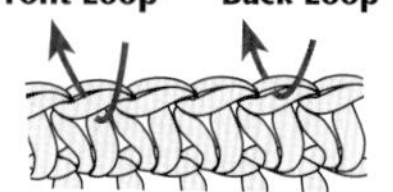

Front post stitch—fp: Back post stitch—bp: When working post st, insert hook from right to left around post st on previous row.

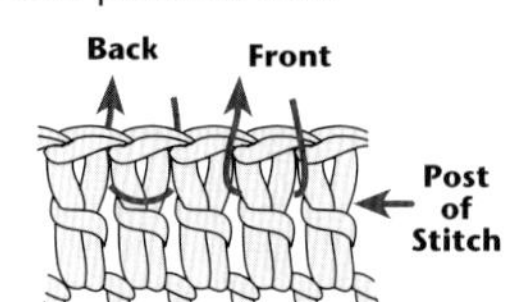

Half double crochet—hdc: Yo, insert hook in st, yo, pull through st, yo, pull through all 3 lps on hook.

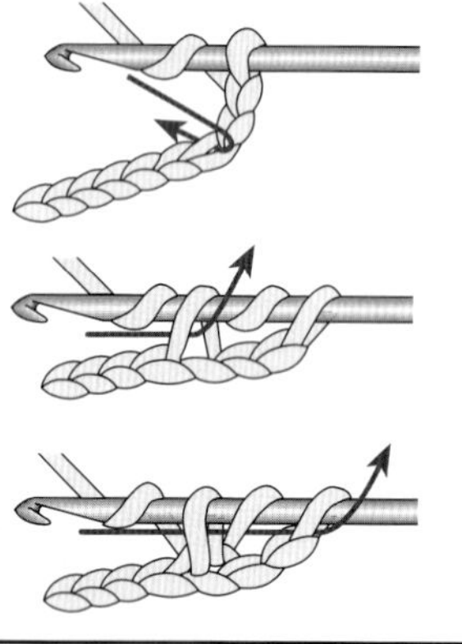

Double crochet—dc: Yo, insert hook in st, yo, pull through st, [yo, pull through 2 lps] twice.

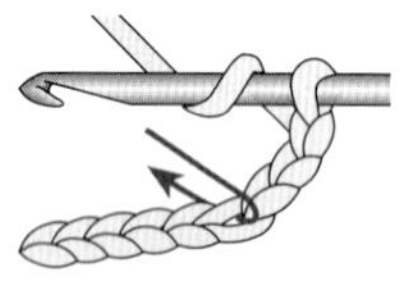
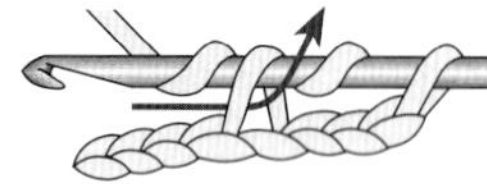
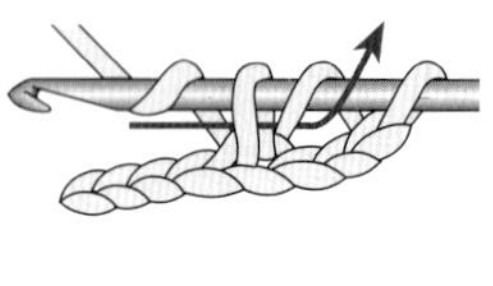
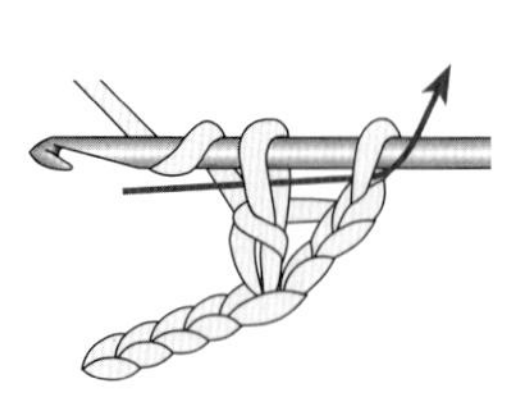

Change colors: Drop first color; with second color, pull through last 2 lps of st.

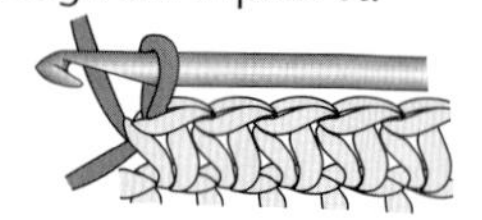

Treble crochet—tr: Yo 2 times, insert hook in st, yo, pull through st, [yo, pull through 2 lps] 3 times.

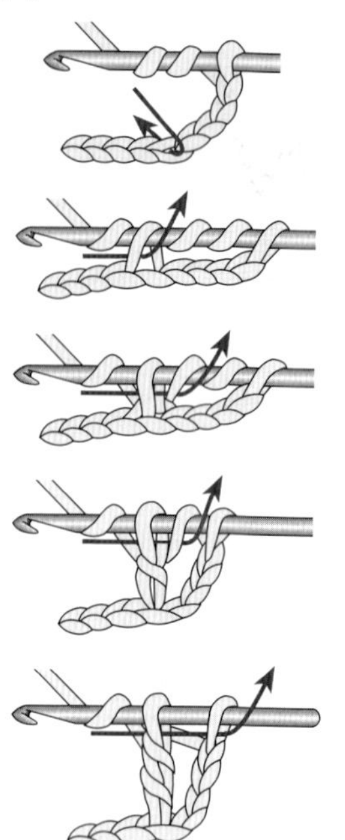

Double treble crochet—dtr: Yo 3 times, insert hook in st, yo, pull through st, [yo, pull through 2 lps] 4 times.

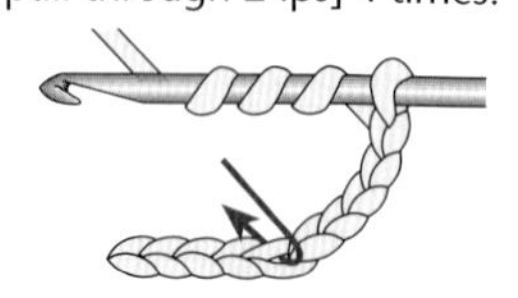

Single crochet decrease (sc dec): (Insert hook, yo, draw up a lp) in each of the sts indicated, yo, draw through all lps on hook.

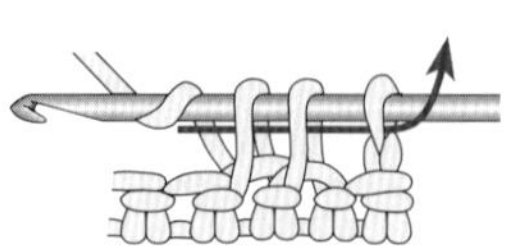
Example of 2-sc dec

Half double crochet decrease (hdc dec): (Yo, insert hook, yo, draw lp through) in each of the sts indicated, yo, draw through all lps on hook.

Example of 2-hdc dec

Double crochet decrease (dc dec): (Yo, insert hook, yo, draw lp through, yo, draw through 2 lps on hook) in each of the sts indicated, yo, draw through all lps on hook.

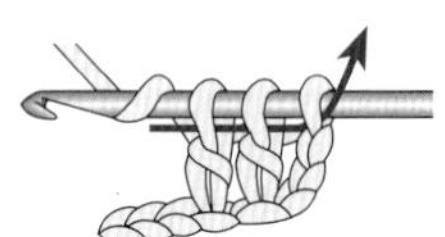
Example of 2-dc dec

US	= UK
sl st (slip stitch)	= sc (single crochet)
sc (single crochet)	= dc (double crochet)
hdc (half double crochet)	= htr (half treble crochet)
dc (double crochet)	= tr (treble crochet)
tr (treble crochet)	= dtr (double treble crochet)
dtr (double treble crochet)	= ttr (triple treble crochet)
skip	= miss

For more complete information, visit

StitchGuide.com